FARMSTAND FAVORITES

Apples

Over 75 Farm Fresh Recipes

Farmstand Favorites: Apples
Text copyright © 2010 Hatherleigh Press

Hatherleigh Press is committed to preserving and protecting the natural resources of the Earth. Environmentally responsible and sustainable practices are embraced within the company's mission statement.

Hatherleigh Press is a member of the Publishers Earth Alliance, committed to preserving and protecting the natural resources of the planet while developing a sustainable business model for the book publishing industry.

This book was edited and designed in the village of Hobart, New York. Hobart is a community that has embraced books and publishing as a component of its livelihood. There are several unique bookstores in the village. For more information, please visit www.hobartbookvillage.com.

www.hatherleighpress.com

DISCLAIMER
This book offers general cooking and eating suggestions for educational purposes only. In no case should it be a substitute nor replace a healthcare professional. Consult your healthcare professional to determine which foods are safe for you and to establish the right diet for your personal nutritional needs.

Library of Congress Cataloging-in-Publication Data

Farmstand favorites. Apples : over 75 farm-fresh recipes.
    p. cm. – (Farmstand favorites)
ISBN 978-1-57826-358-5 (pbk. : alk. paper) 1. Cooking (Apples) I. Hatherleigh Press.
TX813.A6F37 2010
641.3'411–dc22
                                            2010025112

Cover Design by Nick Macagnone
Photography by Catarina Astrom
Interior Design by Nick Macagnone

10 9 8 7 6 5 4 3 2 1

Table of Contents

All About Apples

"An apple a day keeps the doctor away." This saying, which originated from an old English adage, attests to the wealth of advantages gained from eating apples.

The health benefits and many uses of apples have been recognized by people for centuries, tracing as far back as the ancient Romans and Egyptians. They were then introduced to Britain and later brought to America via the Pilgrims, who planted the first American apple trees in the Massachusetts Bay Colony. Today, there are over 2,500 varieties of apples grown in the United States alone and over 7,500 variations grown worldwide. America is now ranked among the top five apple producers worldwide, second only to the Republic of China.

Here is a list of some of the most popular apple varieties in America and the best times of year to find them:

Did you know?

- Apples are grown in the continental U.S. and are commercially grown in 36 states.

- America's top apple producing states are Washington, New York, Virginia, California, Pennsylvania and Michigan.

- **Cortland** – Available September through April

- **Empire** – Available September through July

- **Fuji** – Available year round, beginning in September

- **Gala** – Available year round, beginning in mid-July

- **Golden Delicious** – Available year round, beginning in September

- **Granny Smith** – Available year round, beginning in August

- **Jonagold** – Available October through July

- **McIntosh** – Available September through May

- **Pink Lady** – Available mid-October through June
- **Red Delicious** – Available year round, beginning in September
- **Rome Beauty** – Available late-October through September

Apples are an excellent source of both insoluble and soluble fibers, pectin, antioxidants, flavonoids (which aid in the prevention of heart disease and stroke), over 200 nutrients (such as potassium and phenols), vitamins (especially Vitamin C), and water.

They are also linked to an extensive list of health benefits such as aiding in the treatment and prevention of diabetes and heart disease, as well as several types of cancer (breast, colon, liver, lung, pancreatic, and prostate). Research has shown that consumption of apples helps with brain health, age-related memory loss, and Alzheimer's disease. They also offer a boost in losing weight when combined with a low-calorie diet.

Did you know?

- Apples contain zero fat, cholesterol, or sodium.
- One medium apple is only about 80 calories.
- Most of the antioxidants and two-thirds of the fiber are found in the apple peel.
- Eating a fresh apple eliminates more than 95% of the tooth decay-causing bacteria in your mouth.
- To gain the full benefits of apples, you should eat one each day. The average American consumer only eats about one apple per week.

When selecting the best apples, rely on your senses of touch, smell and sight:

- They should be firm to the touch, with no soft spots.
- Ripe apples have a pleasant aroma.
- Look for apples that do not have bruises, breaks in the skin, or discoloration.

Fresh apples should keep well for up to six weeks if properly stored. Follow these tips:

- Store apples in a cold, humid environment at a temperature around 30-32 °F.

- Keep them in a plastic bag with holes to hold in humidity and avoid a buildup of carbon dioxide in the bag. Lower humidity will remove moisture from the apples and cause them to shrivel.

- Avoid storing apples with onions, potatoes or other pungent herbs and vegetables. They will absorb the flavors.

- Inspect them regularly and remove any apples that are frozen, molding, overripe, or otherwise damaged. This will prevent the others from doing the same.

Breakfast

Golden Apple Oatmeal

Ingredients:

1 Golden Delicious apple, diced
⅓ cup apple juice
⅓ cup water
Dash cinnamon
Dash nutmeg
⅓ cup quick-cook rolled oats, uncooked

Directions:

Combine apples, juice, water and seasonings; bring to a boil. Stir in rolled oats; cook 1 minute. Cover and let stand several minutes before serving.

Swiss Muesli

Ingredients:

1½ cups rolled oats
1½ cups water
2 cups shredded, unpeeled apples
1½ cups (approximately 9 ounces) pitted prunes, whole or halved
2 tablespoons honey

2 tablespoons lemon juice
½ teaspoon cinnamon
3 bananas, sliced
3 oranges, segmented
1 cup chopped almonds

Directions:

Combine oats, water, shredded apples, prunes, honey, lemon juice and cinnamon. Cover and refrigerate overnight. In the morning, spoon some of the muesli into a cereal bowl. Top with your choice of fresh fruits and nuts. Serve with a dollop of plain yogurt or milk, if desired. Muesli can be stored in covered container in refrigerator for several days.

Breakfast Waffle Club Sandwich with Honey Apple Syrup

(Courtesy of the National Honey Board)

Ingredients:

¾ cup honey, divided
¼ cup apple juice
2 tablespoons butter or margarine
2 crisp red apples, cored and sliced
8 frozen waffles, toasted
8 thin slices of ham

Directions:

To prepare syrup, place ½ cup honey and apple juice in small saucepan over medium heat; heat through. Set aside and keep warm. Melt butter with remaining ¼ cup honey in large nonstick skillet over medium-high heat. Add apples; cook, stirring constantly, about 4 minutes or until apples are lightly caramelized, crisp-tender and nicely glazed. For each serving, place 2 waffles on plate, overlapping slightly. Top each waffle with 1 slice ham. Top with ¼ of apple mixture and drizzle with ¼ of syrup.

Avocado and Fruit Salad Topping for Waffles

Ingredients:

2 Red Delicious apples, cut into ½-inch cubes
1 teaspoon lemon juice
2 avocados, cut into ½-inch cubes
2 kiwi fruits, sliced
1 banana sliced
1 pint strawberries, sliced

1 pint blueberries
1 tablespoon honey
¼ teaspoon mace (East Indian spice similar to nutmeg)

Directions:

Place apples in a bowl with lemon juice to keep from browning. Add all other ingredients. Gently mix fruit salad topping. Serve on top of waffles, with or without liquid syrup.

Apple Soufflé

Ingredients:

1 pint steamed apples
1 tablespoon melted butter
½ cup sugar
6 egg whites
3 egg yolks
Nutmeg, freshly grated

Directions:

Stir into the hot apple the butter, sugar and nutmeg and yolks of eggs, well-heated. When this is cold, add the well-beaten whites to the mixture. Butter a 3-pint dish and turn the soufflé into it. Bake thirty minutes in a hot oven. Serve immediately, with any kind of sauce.

Fresh Orange Compote with Granola

Ingredients:
2 navel oranges, peeled, separated into segments
1 apple, diced
½ cup halved seedless red or green grapes
1 banana, peeled, thinly sliced
2 tablespoons fresh squeezed orange juice
½ cup low-fat granola cereal

Directions:
In a medium bowl toss together orange segments, apple, grapes, banana and orange juice. Sprinkle granola over mixture; toss lightly. Serve for breakfast topped with low-fat yogurt.

Sweet Potato Pancakes
with Apple-Walnut Topping

Ingredients:

6 cups sweet potatoes or yams, shredded
¼ cup all-purpose flour
½ teaspoon baking powder
¼ teaspoon ground cinnamon
1 tablespoon honey
1 large egg
2 large egg whites

½ cup light brown sugar, firmly packed
⅓ cup walnuts, chopped
1 tablespoon orange juice
½ teaspoon ground cinnamon
2 baking apples, peeled, cored, and thinly sliced (McIntosh or Cortland will work well)

Directions:

In a large bowl, combine sweet potatoes, flour, baking powder, cinnamon, honey, egg, and egg whites and stir with a fork until mixed well. Coat a large nonstick skillet with cooking spray and place over medium heat. Drop the batter by about 2 tablespoonfuls into hot pan to make several pancakes. Flatten slightly with a spatula until about 3 inches across. Cook the pancakes until golden on both sides. Transfer the pancakes to a warm large plate and keep warm. Repeat with the remaining batter, coating the skillet with cooking spray, as needed.

Topping:

In a large skillet, stir together brown sugar, walnuts, orange juice, and cinnamon. Add the apples and cook over medium-high heat, stirring, until the apples are tender and the brown sugar has melted to form a syrup. Serve with the pancakes.

Apple Omelet

Ingredients:

9 large tart apples
4 eggs
1 cup sugar
1 tablespoon butter
Cinnamon or spices to taste

Directions:

Take nine large, tart apples, four eggs, one cup of sugar, one tablespoonful of butter; add cinnamon or other spices to suit your taste; stew the apples till they are very soft; mash them so that there will be no lumps; add the butter and sugar while they are still warm; but let them cool before putting in the beaten eggs. Bake until it is brown; you may put it all in a shallow dish or in two tin plates to bake.

Ready, Set, Go! French Toast

Ingredients:

1½ cups Granny Smith apples, cored and diced with skin on
3 teaspoons Splenda® No Calorie Sweetener
¼ teaspoon cinnamon
1½ tablespoons skim milk
2 eggs
2 egg whites
3 seconds butter-flavored cooking oil spray
6 slices whole wheat bread
6 tablespoons reduced-calorie syrup

Directions:

In a microwave safe medium sized bowl, combine diced apples, sweetener, and cinnamon. Mix well. Microwave mixture for 1 minute. Beat milk, eggs, and egg whites together in a wide, shallow bowl. Spray cooking pan with cooking oil. Place on burner over medium-high heat. Dip bread into egg batter coating lightly but completely on both sides. Place in pan. Cook turning often until golden brown on both sides. Place two slices of french toast on a plate. Cut each slice of bread in half. Top each serving with diced apple mix and 2 tablespoons of syrup.

Yogurt-Granola Parfait

Ingredients:

1¾ cups plain or vanilla yogurt
6 tablespoons honey
8 ounces fresh berries
(blackberries, blueberries, raspberries and/or strawberries)
2 Cameo apples
2½ cups granola

Directions:

Stir together the yogurt and 4 tablespoons of the honey in a small bowl. Pick over the berries to remove any stems or leaves and halve or quarter larger berries. Put the berries in a medium bowl. Quarter and core the apples and cut them into ¼-inch dice. Stir the apples and the remaining 2 tablespoons of honey into the berries. Spoon a few tablespoons of the granola into the bottom of each sundae dish or wine glass. Top the granola with a few tablespoons of yogurt, then add a generous spoonful of the apple-berry mixture. Repeat the layering 1 more time, drizzling any remaining juice from the fruit over the top.

Apple Loaf

Ingredients:

2 cups flour
2 teaspoons baking powder
1 teaspoon salt
1 tablespoon shortening
1 cup sugar
1 egg
Milk
Apples

Directions:

Mix together flour, baking powder, salt, sugar, and shortening. Break the egg into the flour mixture. Add sufficient milk to make a stiff batter, and pour into a shallow pan. Pare and slice apples, covering the top of the batter with them. When almost done, sprinkle sugar over them.

Soups

Mulligatawny Soup

Ingredients:

Turkey stock
3 apples, finely chopped
2 carrots
1 small onion
3 tablespoons shortening
½ cup flour
1 tablespoon salt
1½ teaspoons paprika
¼ teaspoon nutmeg
½ cup celery, finely chopped
4 tablespoons washed rice

Directions:

Place 4 cups of turkey stock in a saucepan and add apples, carrot, and onion. Bring to a boil and cook slowly until vegetables are soft and then place three tablespoonfuls of shortening in saucepan and add one-half cupful of flour. Stir until well browned and then add two cupfuls of turkey stock. Cook for ten minutes and add to the soup. Bring to a boil, then strain and season with salt, paprika, nutmeg, three pints of turkey stock, chopped celery, one carrot diced, and rice.

Bring to a boil and cook for 35 minutes very slowly and then season.

Curried Butternut Apple Soup

Ingredients:
¼ cup reduced fat margarine
2 cups chopped onion
1 rib celery
4 teaspoons curry powder
2 medium butternut squash (about 2½-3 pounds) peeled, seeded, and cut into cubes
3 medium apples, peeled, cored, and chopped
3 cups water (or chicken stock or vegetable broth)
1 cup cider

Directions:
In a heavy kettle, combine onions, celery, margarine and curry powder. Cover and cook over low heat until vegetables are tender (10-15 minutes), stirring often. Add cubed squash, chopped apples, and liquid (water, stock or broth) and bring to a boil. Reduce heat and simmer 20-30 minutes or until squash and apples are cooked thoroughly. Strain liquid and set aside. Purée the apple-squash mixture with one cup of the strained liquid. Add cider and remaining liquid to reach desired consistency. Garnish with grated apple, yogurt or low-fat sour cream.

Apple Fennel Soup

Ingredients:

2 cups low-sodium chicken broth
2 cups water
½ cup white wine
2 Golden Delicious apples, peeled, cored and chopped
1 cup thinly sliced carrots
1 small onion, thinly sliced
1 cup chopped fennel
1 bay leaf
¼ teaspoon dried thyme leaves
6 peppercorns
4 teaspoons non-fat plain yogurt

Directions:

In large pot, combine broth, water, wine, apples, carrots, onion, fennel, bay leaf, thyme and peppercorns; bring to boil. Reduce heat and simmer, covered, 20 minutes. Strain soup, reserving liquid. Remove bay leaf from apple-vegetable mixture in strainer. In blender or food processor, purée mixture; add reserved liquid and blend well. Reheat soup, if necessary, ladle into soup bowls and serve with a dollop of yogurt if desired.

Creamy Squash Soup
with Shredded Apples
(Courtesy of NHLBI, part of NIH and HHS)

Ingredients:
32 ounces puréed winter (butternut) squash
2 medium apples (try Golden Delicious or Gala)
1 tablespoon olive oil
½ teaspoon pumpkin pie spice
2 (12 oz.) cans fat-free evaporated milk
¼ teaspoon salt
⅛ teaspoon ground black pepper

Directions:
Peel then shred the apples using a grater or food processor, or peel and finely chop apples into thin strips. Set aside ¼ cup. Warm oil in a 4-quart saucepan over medium heat. Add all but ¼ cup of the apples. Cook and stir until apples soften, about 5 minutes. Stir in squash and pumpkin pie spice. Add the evaporated milk about ½ cup at a time, stirring after each addition. Season with salt and pepper. Cook and stir over high heat just until soup is about to boil. Ladle into individual soup bowls. Top each with a tablespoon of the unused apples. Sprinkle with additional pumpkin pie spice, if desired.

Turkey and Cranberry Stew

Ingredients:

2 teaspoons canola oil
1 medium onion, chopped
1 large carrot,
cut into bite-size pieces
1 rib celery, cut into
thin slices
1 parsnip, peeled and
cut into bite-size pieces
(optional)
1 medium sweet potato
or yam, peeled and cut
in half, then into bite-size
pieces
1 bay leaf

1 teaspoon dried thyme
2 cups non-fat, reduced-sodium
turkey or chicken stock, divided
1 sweet, juicy apple, peeled,
cored and cut into bite-size
pieces
1 cup frozen (and defrosted)
cranberries or canned whole
cranberries, rinsed and drained
3 cups diced cooked turkey
Salt and freshly ground black
pepper, to taste

Directions:

In a deep pan or skillet, heat the oil over medium-high heat. Sauté the onion until it softens, about 4 minutes. Add the carrot, celery, parsnip (if using) and sweet potato. Lower heat to medium and, stirring frequently, saute until the vegetables become lightly browned. Add the bay leaf, thyme and 1 cup of stock. Lower heat to a simmer and cook until the vegetables are almost tender, about 10 minutes or less. Stir in the apple and cranberries, if using the frozen kind. If the mixture seems dry, add enough additional stock to cook the fruit. Gently simmer until the apple has softened and the cranberries are tender, about 5 minutes. If using canned cranberries, add them after the apple has softened, along with the turkey. Heat through for a few more minutes, until the turkey is hot. Season to taste with salt and pepper. Serve as is or over cooked brown rice or whole-grain pasta, if desired.

Cheddar Soup with Granny Smith Apples

Ingredients:

3 tablespoons unsalted butter
1 large onion, diced
⅓ cup all-purpose flour
2 teaspoons mustard powder
4 cups chicken broth
2 Granny Smith apples
1 cup apple cider or apple juice
10 ounces sharp cheddar cheese, grated (about 3½ cups)
Salt and freshly ground black pepper
Few dashes Tabasco sauce

Directions:

Melt the butter in a large saucepan over medium heat. Add the onion and sauté until tender and aromatic, 5 to 7 minutes. Sprinkle the flour and mustard powder over the onion and stir to evenly coat. Continue cooking, stirring often, for 1 to 2 minutes. Add the broth, stirring until well blended. Peel, quarter and core 1 of the Granny Smith apples and finely chop it. Add the apple to the soup, cover the pan, reduce the heat to low and simmer until the soup is thickened and the apple is tender, about 10 minutes. Stir in the cider and grated cheese and cook a few minutes longer, stirring constantly, until the cheese is fully melted. Using a blender, purée the soup until smooth. Stir in the Tabasco sauce with salt and pepper to taste. Quarter and core the remaining Granny Smith apple and cut it into ½-inch dice. Ladle the soup into warmed bowls, scatter the apple over and serve right away.

Watermelon-Apple Gazpacho

Ingredients:

6 cups watermelon, seeded and cubed
1½ cups (2 medium) Golden Delicious apples, cored and chopped
½ cup (1 medium) onion, finely chopped
½ cup green bell pepper, finely chopped
1 teaspoon dried basil
½ teaspoon salt
¼ teaspoon black pepper, coarsely ground
¼ teaspoon chili powder
1 tablespoon cider vinegar

Directions:

In a blender, purée the watermelon until smooth; pour into a
large bowl. Stir in the remaining ingredients.

Cover and refrigerate at least 2 hours, or until well chilled.

Salads

Apple-Hazelnut Salad in a Cup

Ingredients:

2 tablespoons non-fat bottled raspberry vinaigrette
1 apple, diced
¼ cup dried fruit tidbits
2 tablespoons chopped hazelnuts
1 cup pre-cut mixed greens, rinsed and drained

Directions:

Layer ingredients, in order, in a large, travel-proof, lidded, insulated cup. When ready to eat, grab a fork and shake the cup well. Enjoy!

Apple, Date and Orange Salad

Ingredients:
1 cup diced apples
¾ cup dates, seeded
2 oranges
Lettuce
Salad dressing

Directions:
Peel the apples and dice them into fine pieces. Wash the dates, remove the seeds, and cut each date into six or eight pieces. Prepare the oranges as directed for preparing oranges for salad, and cut each section into two or three pieces. Just before serving, mix the fruits carefully so as not to make the salad look mushy, pile in a neat heap on garnished salad plates, and serve with any desired dressing.

Green Apple and Onion Salad

Ingredients:

2 Granny Smith apples (about 1 pound) quartered lengthwise, cored and thinly sliced crosswise

1 small Vidalia or white onion, quartered and thinly sliced

1-inch piece ginger, peeled and cut into very fine matchsticks

2 tablespoons finely shredded fresh basil

3 tablespoons fresh lemon juice

⅛ teaspoon salt

⅛ teaspoon ground pepper

Directions:

Toss apple slices with lemon juice to prevent browning. Mix all ingredients in a bowl and serve.

Apple Carrot Salad

Ingredients:

1 cup shredded carrot

3 (medium) unpared and diced apples

1 tablespoon lemon juice

½ cup raisins

⅓ cup low-fat mayonnaise

Directions:

Combine all ingredients. Chill thoroughly. Serve on salad greens.

Autumn Salad

(Courtesy of NHLBI, part of NIH and HHS)

Ingredients:

1 Granny Smith apple, rinsed and sliced thinly (with skin)
2 tablespoons lemon juice
1 bag mixed lettuce greens (or your favorite lettuce,
about 5 cups), rinsed
½ cup dried cranberries
¼ cup walnuts, chopped
¼ cup unsalted sunflower seeds
⅓ cup low-fat raspberry vinaigrette dressing

Directions:

Sprinkle lemon juice on the apple slices. Mix the lettuce, cranberries, apple, walnuts, and sunflower seeds in a bowl. Toss with
raspberry vinaigrette dressing, to lightly cover the salad, and
serve.

Honeyed Fuji Apple Pasta Salad
(Courtesy of the National Honey Board)

Ingredients:
16 ounces small shell pasta, dry
¾ cup honey
¾ cup mayonnaise
½ cup lemon juice
¼ cup Dijon mustard
½ teaspoon salt
¼ cup parsley, stems removed
1½ teaspoons dried thyme
2 Fuji apples, cored and chopped in ¼-inch dice
2½ cups fully cooked boneless ham, chopped in ¼-inch dice
¾ cup celery, chopped in ¼-inch dice
½ cup coarsely chopped walnuts, toasted

Directions:
Cook pasta according to package directions; drain very well and set aside to cool. Meanwhile, make dressing: Put honey, mayonnaise, lemon juice, mustard and salt in blender jar and whirl on medium for 1 minute or until smooth and creamy. Add parsley and thyme; pulse to chop herbs. In large bowl, gently toss together pasta, apples, ham, celery and dressing. Cover and chill for one hour. Stir in walnuts and serve.

Cabbage and Carrot Salad

Ingredients:
2 cups shredded cabbage
½ cup grated carrot
1 apple, diced
lettuce or cabbage leaves

Dressing:
1¼ teaspoons salt
⅛ teaspoon pepper
Few grains cayenne
½ cup salad oil
2 tablespoons vinegar
¼ cup chili sauce
½ teaspoon table sauce

Directions:
Toss together shredded cabbage, grated carrot and diced apple.
Serve in nests of lettuce or cabbage leaves with Thousand Island
French Dressing.

Dressing:

Mix all ingredients.

Just before serving, add ⅓ cup cream beaten stiff, and shake
thoroughly.

Beet and Apple Salad

Ingredients:
2 cups apples, diced
2 cups cooked beets, diced
¼ cup chopped nuts
2 hard boiled eggs
½ cup salad dressing
Parsley

Dressing:
2 hard boiled eggs, mashed
Grated onion
3 tablespoons salad oil
1 tablespoon vinegar
½ teaspoon salt
Pinch of pepper

Directions:
Mix the apples, beets, and chopped eggs.

Dressing:

Mix well together. Then put on salad, and turn and stir until it is well covered with the dressing. Garnish with chopped nuts and parsley.

Greens with Pineapple, Apple, and Feta

Ingredients:

3 tablespoons balsamic vinegar
3 tablespoons water
2 tablespoons honey mustard
1 clove garlic, minced
6 cups (about 1 head) Boston lettuce leaves, torn
1½ cups canned pineapple chunks in 100% juice, drained
2 medium Red Delicious apples, cored and thinly sliced
1 small red onion, thinly sliced
3 tablespoons feta cheese, crumbled
Black pepper, freshly ground to taste

Directions:

In a small bowl whisk together the vinegar, water, mustard, and garlic; season with pepper, if desired. In a large salad bowl, toss the remaining ingredients. Drizzle the vinaigrette on top and toss gently until evenly coated.

Gingered Sweet Potato-Apple Salad

Ingredients:
15 ounces sweet potatoes or yams, cubed
8 ounces pineapple tidbits, drained
1 apple, cored and diced
½ cup diced celery
½ cup coarsely chopped cashews
¼ cup honey mustard dressing
2 teaspoons freshly grated ginger
6 cups mixed salad greens

Directions:
Combine sweet potatoes, pineapple, apple, celery and cashews
in a large bowl. In a small bowl, combine honey mustard salad
dressing and ginger; pour over sweet potato mixture; toss
lightly.

Cover and chill for at least 1 hour. Serve over salad greens.

Apple and Bow Tie Salad

Ingredients:

1 cup bowtie pasta, dry
1 large apple
2 tablespoons orange juice
¼ cup shredded cheddar cheese, reduced fat
12 cherry tomatoes cut in half
4 cups romaine lettuce
⅓ cup light ranch salad dressing

Directions:

Bring medium size pot of water to boil and add bowtie pasta.
Simmer 11 minutes until pasta is tender. Drain pasta and cool.
Cut apple in quarters. Remove core and slice into ¼-inch pieces.
Place sliced apples into small bowl, add orange juice and stir so
juice covers all apple slices. This keeps the apples from turning
brown. Shred cheese. Cut tomatoes into halves. In large salad
bowl, add romaine lettuce, tomatoes, apples with juice, cheese
and pasta. Add dressing and toss, coating all ingredients. Serve
chilled.

Dilled Granny Apple Chicken Salad

Ingredients:
2 boneless, skinless chicken breast, halved
2 Granny Smith apples, cored and chopped
2 stalks celery, sliced
1 halved seedless green grapes
½ cup low-fat mayonnaise
2 tablespoons chopped fresh dill
1 tablespoon fresh lemon juice
½ cup pistachio nuts, shelled
¼ teaspoon salt
Freshly ground black pepper
Boston lettuce leaves

Directions:
Place chicken breasts on a microwave-safe plate and cover with
wax paper. Microwave on high for 5 minutes, rotating chicken
halfway through cooking, or until chicken is cooked through.
When cool enough to handle, cut chicken into bite-size chunks. In
large bowl, combine chicken, apples, celery, grapes, mayonnaise,
dill, lemon juice, nuts, salt and pepper to taste until well mixed.

Serving Suggestion: Arrange lettuce leaves on platter, top with
apple-chicken salad.

Avocado and Smoked Turkey Salad in Bread Baskets

Ingredients:

¼ cup olive oil
3 tablespoons balsamic vinegar
1 tablespoon orange
marmalade or preserves
1 clove garlic, finely chopped
½ teaspoon curry powder
¼ teaspoon salt
¼ teaspoon black pepper,
freshly ground
2 loaves French bread
(each 12-inches long)
2 tablespoons olive oil
2 tablespoons balsamic vinegar

8 cups mixed baby salad greens
1 cup smoked deli turkey
breast, cubed
1 cup papaya, peeled, seeded,
and cubed
1 cup red or green grapes,
halved if large
1 medium red apple, cored and
cubed
1 ripe avocado, cut into thin
wedges

Directions:

Dressing:

In a small bowl, whisk together the oil, vinegar, marmalade or
preserves, garlic, curry powder, salt, and pepper until blended.
Set aside.

Bread baskets:

Preheat oven to 375°F. Using a serrated knife, cut a 1-inch slice
off the top of each loaf of bread. Cut all around the cut side of
the bread, ½-inch from the edge. With your fingers, rip out the
soft bread to form a ½-inch-thick shell. Repeat with second loaf
of bread. In a small bowl, whisk together the oil and vinegar.
Brush on the inside of each loaf. Place the bread directly on the
oven rack and bake for 5 minutes. Remove from the oven and
cool.

Salad:

Meanwhile, in a large bowl, combine the salad greens, turkey,
papaya, grapes, and apple. Re-whisk the dressing, pour over
the salad, and toss until evenly coated. Spoon the salad into the
bread baskets and top with the avocado wedges. Cut each bread
basket into four portions and serve.

Asian Apple-Chicken Salad

Ingredients:

2 cups cooked chicken breast, cubed

2 cups apples, cored and cubed

2 tablespoons apple, orange, or carrot juice

2 tablespoons lime juice

1 tablespoon sesame oil

1 tablespoon mirin (rice wine)

1 tablespoon low-sodium soy sauce

1 tablespoon fresh ginger, finely grated

¼ cup fresh parsley, chopped

¼ cup fresh cilantro, chopped

3 scallions, thinly sliced

1 pound baby spinach

pepper to taste, if desired

Directions:

Place the chicken and apples in a large bowl. Mix the apple juice, lime juice, sesame oil, mirin, soy sauce and ginger together in a small bowl; pour mixture over the chicken and apples. Sprinkle the parsley, cilantro, and scallions over the top and gently toss to mix. (Cover and refrigerate up to several hours, if desired.) To serve, layer the spinach on a platter and spoon the chicken mixture on top.

Apple and Cucumber Salad

Ingredients:

1 tablespoon sesame seeds
⅓ cup vegetable oil
3 tablespoons rice wine vinegar
1 teaspoon sesame oil
1 teaspoon finely grated fresh ginger
2 Fuji apples
1 large cucumber, peeled, seeded and thinly sliced
Salt

Directions:

Put the sesame seeds in a small dry skillet and lightly toast
them over medium heat, stirring often, 3 to 5 minutes; set aside.
Combine the vegetable oil, rice wine vinegar, sesame oil and ginger in a large bowl and whisk to blend. Season to taste with salt.
Quarter and core the Fuji apples and cut them into thin slices.
Add them to the dressing with the cucumber slices. Toss gently
to evenly mix. Cover with plastic and refrigerate for at least 30
minutes and up to 2 hours before serving, stirring once or twice.
To serve, arrange the salad on individual plates, drizzling a bit
of the dressing over each. Sprinkle the toasted sesame seeds
over and serve.

Meat & Poultry Entrées

Roast Pork Loin with Apples and Cinnamon

(Courtesy of the National Honey Board)

Ingredients:

1½ pounds boneless pork loin
1 tablespoon olive oil
1 teaspoon ground black pepper
1 teaspoon ground ginger
½ teaspoon nutmeg
½ teaspoon cinnamon
½ cup dry white table wine
¼ cup honey
1 tablespoon lemon juice
2 apples, cored, peeled and sliced into wedges

Directions:

Rub pork loin with olive oil, pepper, half of ginger, nutmeg and cinnamon. Combine remaining half of spices with wine, lemon juice and honey; stir in apple wedges. Preheat oven to 350°F. Place pork in shallow baking pan. Roast to an internal temperature of 155°F, about 40 minutes. Remove from oven, cover and keep warm; let rest for 10-15 minutes. Reserve all juices. Heat apple mixture to a boil. Reduce heat to a simmer. Cover and simmer until apples are tender, about 5 minutes. Add any pork juices, simmer a few minutes more. Remove from heat. Slice pork loin; arrange on plates, pour warm sauce over slices, garnish with apples.

Pork Medallions
with Honey-Glazed Fruit

Ingredients:

1 tablespoon vegetable oil
1 tablespoon onion powder
1¾ teaspoon dried thyme
1 teaspoon black pepper,
freshly ground
¾ teaspoon salt
1 pound pork tenderloin,
trimmed and cut into ¾-inch
thick slices

2 large green apples, such as
Granny Smith
2 teaspoons vegetable oil
1 cup dried figs, halved
½ cup dry white wine or water
3 tablespoons honey
Fresh parsley, chopped, for
garnish

Directions:

In a cup, stir together the oil, onion powder, thyme, pepper, and
salt until blended. Rub on both sides of the pork slices. Peel,
core, and cut each apple into 16 wedges. In a large skillet, heat
the oil over medium-high heat until hot. Add the pork and cook
for about 2 minutes on each side, or until lightly browned and
no longer pink. Reduce the heat to medium-low and cook for 3 to
4 minutes longer, or until firm and slightly pink inside. Transfer
the pork to a platter and keep warm. Add the apples, figs, and
wine to the pan. Reduce the heat to medium and cook for about
8 minutes, or until the liquid evaporates, stirring frequently
with a wooden spoon and scraping up the browned bits from the
bottom of the pan. Add the honey and stir for about 2 minutes,
or until the apples are tender and glazed. Spoon the apple-fig
mixture over and around the pork, sprinkle with parsley, and
serve.

Pork Mignons with French Applesauce

(Courtesy of NHLBI, part of NIH and HHS)

Ingredients:

1 pair pork tenderloins
(about 2 pounds)
¼ teaspoon salt
⅛ teaspoon ground black pepper
2 medium apples, rinsed and cored,
but not peeled (try Golden Delicious
or Rome)
2 tablespoons dark seedless raisins
2 tablespoons walnuts, broken into
coarse pieces
½ teaspoon cinnamon
Cooking spray

Also try doubling the sauce to serve over whole-wheat pancakes, or eat alone for dessert.

Directions:

Preheat oven broiler on high temperature, with the rack 3 inches from heat source.

Cover broiler pan with aluminum foil for easy cleanup. Spray foil lightly with cooking spray. Set aside.

Cut 8 slices (pork rounds), each 1½-inch thick, from the center of the pair of pork tenderloins. Refrigerate or freeze the ends for another use. Place pork rounds on the foil-covered broiler pan. Sprinkle with salt and pepper. Set aside a few minutes while broiler heats.

Meanwhile, heat ½ cup water to boiling in a medium nonstick pan. Slice cored apples from top to bottom in ¼-inch wide pieces. Add apples, raisins, walnuts, and cinnamon to boiling water. Reduce heat to medium. Cover. Simmer, stirring occasionally, until apples are soft and easily pierced with a fork. Set aside until pork is cooked.

Broil pork tenderloins for 5-10 minutes per side (for a minimum internal temperature of 160°F).

To serve, place two pork rounds on each dinner plate. Top with ¼ of the applesauce.

Braised Chicken with Apples and Tarragon

Ingredients:

1 chicken (4 to 5 pounds),
cut into 8 pieces, skin on
½ cup all-purpose flour
2 Gala apples
3 tablespoons olive oil
1 large onion, finely chopped
2 tablespoons minced fresh tarragon
¾ cup chicken broth
½ cup dry white wine
Salt and freshly ground black pepper

Simple steamed rice
or mashed potatoes
would be an ideal
accompaniment.

Directions:

Season the chicken pieces with salt and pepper. Put the flour on a plate and use it to coat the chicken pieces, patting to remove excess. Quarter and core the Gala apples and cut them into 1-inch wedges. Heat the oil in a large, deep skillet over medium heat. Brown the chicken pieces on all sides, 5 to 7 minutes total; cook chicken in two batches if needed so pan is not crowded. Set the chicken aside on a plate. Increase the heat to medium-high, add the apple wedges to the skillet and lightly brown them, 3 to 5 minutes. Scoop the apples into a bowl. Add the onion to the skillet and sauté until beginning to soften, stirring occasionally, 2 to 3 minutes. Stir in the tarragon, then add the broth and wine with a good pinch each of salt and pepper. Bring the liquids just to a boil, then reduce the heat to low. Return the chicken pieces to the skillet, cover the pan and simmer gently for 15 minutes. Scatter the apple wedges over the chicken, cover the pan and continue simmering until the chicken is cooked through and tender, about 20 minutes longer, turning the chicken pieces once or twice. Transfer the chicken to a plate and cover with foil to keep warm. Bring the cooking liquids to a boil and reduce slightly to thicken, 3 to 5 minutes. Arrange the chicken pieces and apple wedges on individual plates, spoon the sauce over and serve.

Apple Chicken Stir-Fry

Ingredients:

1 pound cubed boneless, skinless, chicken breast
½ cup onion, vertically sliced
1 ¾ cups (3-4 medium) carrots, thinly sliced
1 ½ teaspoon vegetable oil
1 teaspoon dried basil, crushed
1 cup fresh or frozen Chinese pea pods
1 tablespoon water
1 medium baking apple, cored and thinly sliced
1 tablespoon oil
2 cups cooked brown rice

Directions:

Stir-fry cubed chicken breast in 1 tablespoon vegetable oil in nonstick skillet until lightly browned and cooked. Remove from skillet. Stir-fry onion, carrots and basil in oil in same skillet until carrots are tender. Stir in pea pods and water; stir-fry 2 minutes. Remove from heat; stir in apple. Add to chicken, serve hot over cooked rice.

Turkey-Apple Gyros

Ingredients:

1 medium Golden Delicious apple, cored and thinly sliced

2 tablespoons fresh lemon juice

1 cup thinly sliced onion

1 medium red bell pepper, cut into thin strips

1 medium green bell pepper, cut into thin strips

1 teaspoon olive oil

8 ounces cooked turkey breast, cut into thin strips

6 whole wheat pita bread rounds, lightly toasted

½ cup plain low-fat yogurt

1 garlic clove, minced

Directions:

Toss apple with lemon juice; set aside. In a large nonstick skillet, saute onion and peppers in hot oil, stirring frequently until crisp-tender. Add turkey to skillet and stir until heated through. Stir in apple mixture. Add garlic to yogurt and mix. Fold pitas in half and fill with turkey mixture. Drizzle with yogurt mixture.

Spanish Hot Dish Dinner

Ingredients:

¾ pound ground turkey meat
1 cup chopped onion
2 garlic cloves, minced
1 (14½ oz.) can no added salt whole tomatoes, undrained and chopped
1 (4 oz.) can diced green chilies, drained
⅓ cup raisins
½ teaspoon salt
½ teaspoon pepper

½ teaspoon cinnamon
¼ teaspoon cloves
¼ teaspoon allspice
¼ teaspoon nutmeg
¼ teaspoon orange rind
½ teaspoon hot sauce
1 cup canned black beans, rinsed and drained
2 cups finely chopped apple
3 cups cooked brown rice
Nonstick cooking spray

Directions:

Cook turkey meat over medium heat until browned, stirring to crumble. Drain any juices and pat dry with paper towels and set aside. Wipe drippings from skillet and coat with cooking spray; place over medium heat until hot. Add onion and garlic; sauté 2 minutes or until tender. Return turkey meat to skillet. Add tomatoes, green chiles, raisins, salt, pepper, spices, orange rind and hot sauce. Bring to boil, then reduce heat to simmer, uncovered, for 15 minutes. Add beans and apple. Cook for 10 minutes, stirring occasionally. Serve over rice.

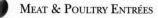

Broiled Sirloin with Spicy Mustard and Apple Chutney

(Courtesy of NHLBI, part of NIH and HHS)

Ingredients:

Chutney

1 Granny Smith apple, rinsed, peeled, cored, and diced (about 1 cup)

2 tablespoons shallots, minced

1 tablespoon garlic, minced (about 2–3 cloves)

½ cup canned no-salt-added diced tomatoes

2 ounces golden seedless raisins (about ½ cup)

¼ cup apple cider vinegar

2 tablespoons maple syrup

Steaks

4 beef top sirloin steaks, lean (3 ounces each)

¼ teaspoon salt

¼ teaspoon ground black pepper

1 tablespoon olive oil

Mustard Dressing

2 cups low-sodium beef broth

2 tablespoons Dijon mustard

2 tablespoons cornstarch

Directions:

Chutney

Combine all the ingredients in a small saucepan. Bring to a boil over high heat, and simmer for 20 minutes or until apples are cooked and soft. Remove from the heat and hold warm, or cool and store.

Steaks

Preheat grill pan or oven broiler (with the rack 3 inches from heat source) on high temperature. Season the steaks with salt and pepper, and lightly coat with oil. Grill or broil 3–4 minutes on each side, or to your desired doneness (to a minimum internal temperature of 145˚F). Remove from the heat and set aside for 5 minutes.

Mustard Dressing

Mix together beef broth, Dijon mustard, and cornstarch in a small saucepan. Bring to a boil on medium-high heat while stirring constantly. Lower the heat, and simmer for 2–3 minutes.

Serve each steak with ¼ cup of chutney and ½ cup of mustard dressing.

Hanukkah Rack of Lamb
(Courtesy of the National Honey Board)

Ingredients:

1 8-rib rack of lamb
2 tablespoons olive oil
½ teaspoon black pepper
¼ teaspoon salt
¼ cup honey
1 tablespoon lemon juice
1 tablespoon brown sugar
1 teaspoon Dijon mustard
½ cup dried apricots, diced
½ cup prunes, diced

½ cup apples, diced
½ cup burgundy wine
1 tablespoon vinegar
1 tablespoon lemon juice
1 tablespoon honey
¼ teaspoon allspice
¼ teaspoon cinnamon

Directions:

Rub rack with olive oil and sprinkle with salt and pepper. Combine honey, lemon juice, brown sugar and mustard. Baste rack with honey mixture. Roast rack in 400°F oven for 15 to 20 minutes or until medium rare. Continue to baste rack with honey glaze. Meanwhile, prepare Fruit Sauce by combining remaining ingredients and simmering for 20 minutes. When rack is done, let rest for 50 to 10 minutes before carving. Serve with fruit sauce.

Honey-Curry Ham and Apple Pockets

(Courtesy of the National Honey Board)

Ingredients:

2 quarts (2 pounds, 8 ounces) onion, chopped
3 quarts (4 pounds) apples, peeled, chopped coarsely
½ cup vegetable oil
1¼ gallon (4 pounds) ham, diced
2½ tablespoons curry powder
2⅝ cups (2 pounds) honey
8 ounces frozen bread dough, thawed
1½ cups whipping cream

Directions:

Sauté onion and apple in oil until soft, about 10 minutes. Stir in ham and curry powder; stir in honey. Cool to room temperature. Reserve. Scale dough into 24 pieces, 3 ounces each; roll each into a circle about 7" in diameter. Place ½ cup reserved filling on half of circle; fold other half over. Tightly seal edges, then flute; put on a parchment lined sheet pan. Repeat with remaining ingredients. Brush top of each pastry with cream. Bake at 450°F until browned, about 15 minutes. Remove from oven; cool. Serve warm or at room temperature. Refrigerate turnovers.

Vegetarian Entrées

Celery and Apple Steam-Fry with Honey-Mustard Sauce

Ingredients:

1 cup water
4 cups celery, diagonally sliced ½-inch thick
2 cups diced sweet red apples (approximately 2 medium)
2 tablespoons Dijon-style mustard
1 tablespoon honey
1 teaspoon cornstarch
⅛ teaspoon ground black pepper
¼ cup chopped and toasted walnuts

Directions:

In a large skillet bring water to a boil. Add celery and apples; cook and stir until crisp-tender, about 8 minutes. In a small bowl combine mustard, honey, cornstarch and black pepper with 2 Tbsp water. Add to celery mixture, stirring constantly; cook and stir until clear and thickened, about 1 minute. Stir in walnuts, if desired. Serve over rice.

Spicy Apple-Filled Squash

Ingredients:

1 acorn squash (about 1 pound)
1 Golden Delicious apple, peeled, cored and sliced
2 teaspoons reduced-fat margarine, melted
2 teaspoons brown sugar
⅛ teaspoon cinnamon
⅛ teaspoon nutmeg
Dash ground cloves

Directions:

Heat oven to 350°F. Grease a 1-quart baking dish. Halve squash and remove seeds; cut into quarters. Place quarters, skin side up, in dish and cover; bake 30 minutes. Meanwhile, in medium bowl, combine apple, butter, brown sugar, cinnamon, nutmeg, and cloves. Turn cut sides of acorn squash up; top with apple mixture. Cover and bake 30 minutes longer or until apples are tender. Variations: Quick microwave version Halve and seed squash; cut into quarters. Arrange quarters, cut side up, in microwave-safe baking dish. Microwave on high (100 percent) 6 to 7 minutes, rotating squash halfway through cooking time. Top squash with apple mixture, cover with vented plastic wrap and microwave on high 4 to 5 minutes or until apples are tender.

Fruity Curried Lentils

Ingredients:
2 cups uncooked lentils
2 quarts water
2 apples cored peeled and chopped
¼ cup golden raisins
¼ cup non-fat lemon yogurt
1 teaspoon curry powder
½ teaspoon salt

Directions:
Combine lentils and water in a large saucepan. Bring to a boil over high heat. Reduce heat and simmer 20 minutes, stirring occasionally. Stir apples and raisins into saucepan; cook 10 minutes or until lentils are tender. Drain well. Place lentil mixture in large serving bowl. Stir in yogurt, curry powder, and salt until well blended.

Scalloped Sweet Potatoes and Apples

Ingredients:
6 medium-sized sweet potatoes
½ cup brown sugar
1½ cups sliced apples
4 tablespoons butter
½ teaspoon salt
1 teaspoon mace (East Indian spice similar to nutmeg)

Directions:
Boil sweet potatoes until tender. Slice in ¼-inch pieces. Butter baking dish and put a layer of sweet potatoes in bottom, then a layer of apples. Sprinkle with sugar, salt and mace, and dot with butter. Repeat until dish is filled, having the top layer of apples. Bake in moderate oven (350°F) for 50 minutes.

Honey Noodle Kugel

(Courtesy of the National Honey Board)

Ingredients:

8 ounces medium noodles
¼ cup butter or margarine, melted
4 eggs, lightly beaten
½ cup honey
½ cup raisins
4 apples, coarsely grated
1 teaspoon salt
1 teaspoon ground cinnamon

Crisp Topping
⅓ cup bread crumbs
1 teaspoon ground cinnamon
¼ cup honey

Directions:

Cook noodles according to package directions. Drain and place in large bowl. Add butter; mix well. Cool 10 minutes. Add eggs, honey, raisins, apples, salt and cinnamon; mix well. Place noodle mixture in greased 9-inch square baking pan. Top with Crisp Topping and cover with foil. Bake at 350°F for 50 minutes. Uncover and bake 10 to 15 minutes more or until browned on top.

Crisp Topping

Combine bread crumbs and cinnamon; mix well. Drizzle honey over mixture and stir until crumbs are coated. Makes ⅓ cup.

Sauce à la Bonne Femme

Ingredients:

2 tomatoes
1 green apple
1 leek
2 ounces butter
1 teaspoon lemon juice
½ pint lentil or haricot bean stock
½ teaspoon mixed herbs
Salt and pepper to taste

Directions:

Dissolve the butter in a small pan, then place in the vegetables sliced, and fry for twenty minutes, but do not allow to burn; add stock, lemon juice, salt and pepper, and simmer for half an hour. Strain before using. May be thickened if required.

Serve over fried beans, lentils, or potatoes.

Honey-Roasted Parsnips

Ingredients:
1½ cups parsnips, peeled and cut into bite-size chunks
1 large sweet potato, peeled and cut into bite-size chunks
2 firm Gala or Fuji apples, peeled, cored and cut into bite-size chunks
1 tablespoon canola oil
1 tablespoon honey
1 tablespoon balsamic vinegar

Directions:
Preheat oven to 375°F. Coat a casserole dish with canola oil spray and set aside. In a large mixing bowl, place the parsnips, sweet potatoes and apples and set aside. In a microwave-proof bowl, mix together the canola oil and honey. Place in a microwave and warm for 10 seconds. Mix in balsamic vinegar. Pour onto vegetables and apples. Toss to coat well. Transfer to casserole dish, cover and bake until tender, about 1 hour.

Side Dishes & Snacks

Roast Celery with Apples

Ingredients:

1 large clove garlic, crushed
2 tablespoons olive oil
1 stalk celery, about 1½ pounds
2 Golden Delicious apples, cored and quartered
1 cup apple juice
¼ teaspoon ground cinnamon
¼ teaspoon salt
⅛ teaspoon ground black pepper
4 slices toasted Italian bread

Directions:

Preheat oven to 375°F. Place garlic and oil in a 13 x 9 x 2-inch baking pan; bake until oil is hot, about 5 minutes. Meanwhile trim base of celery; cut celery stalk crosswise, about 7 inches from base (save top for soups, stews, etc); cut stalk lengthwise into 4 wedges. Place celery, apples, apple juice, cinnamon, salt and pepper in baking pan; bake, uncovered, until celery is crisp-tender, about 40 minutes, basting with pan juices every 10 to 15 minutes; discard garlic. Serve immediately over Italian bread.

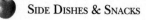

String Beans and Apples

Ingredients:

String beans, broken in small pieces
Apples, pared and quartered
1 tablespoon flour
1 tablespoon butter
3 tablespoons vinegar
Lemon, thinly sliced
Salt to taste

Directions:

Take three parts of string beans to one part apples. Break the beans into small pieces, pare and quarter the apples. Boil the beans in salted water until soft, and drain. Mix a tablespoon each of butter and flour in a saucepan, and add to this three tablespoons each of vinegar and water and season with salt. Pour over the beans and let cook until they are well seasoned. Boil the apples and add thin slices of lemon. When all is ready add the apples to the beans without too much juice. Serve either hot or cold.

Apple Stuffing

Ingredients:

½ pint unsweetened fresh applesauce
½ cup bread crumbs
Powdered sage
Small chopped onion
Cayenne pepper

Directions:

Mix together ½ pint of apple sauce (unsweetened), bread crumbs, some powdered sage, a little chopped onion, and season with cayenne pepper. Delicious for stuffing roast geese, ducks, Cornish hen, or turkey.

Northwest Bruschetta
(Courtesy of the National Honey Board)

Ingredients:

4 Fuji apples
2 teaspoons vegetable oil
¼ cup balsamic vinegar
½ cup honey
32 ½-inch thick slices baguette (about 2 inches diameter)
Olive oil cooking spray
16 very thin slices prosciutto ham (about 10 ounces)
Fresh sage, for garnish

Directions:

Peel and core apples. Cut each apple into 16 wedges. In large
nonstick skillet over medium heat, warm oil and sauté apples 3
minutes or until crisp tender. Add vinegar and cook 3 minutes
or until most of the vinegar is evaporated. Add honey and increase heat to high. When honey bubbles, stir gently for 1 minute until apples are soft. Allow apples to cool in honey syrup.
With a slotted spoon remove apples; discard syrup. Heat oven
to 400°F. Arrange bread slices on wire rack over cookie sheet.
Spray both sides of bread with cooking spray; bake 6 minutes or
until edges of bread are golden brown. Remove and arrange on
serving platter. Immediately before serving, cut each prosciutto
slice into 2- x 1-inch strips. Place one slice of prosciutto on each
toast; top with two apple slices. Garnish with fresh sage.

Citrus Slaw

Ingredients:

¼ cup fat-free herb vinaigrette
2 ounces frozen orange juice concentrate, thawed
4 cups shredded cabbage
2 oranges, sectioned
1 small red apple, halved, cored, and sliced
1 cup (6 ounces) dried plums, pitted, and quartered
½ cup (1 medium stalk) celery, sliced
¼ cup scallions, sliced
Black pepper, freshly ground (optional)

Directions:

In a large bowl, whisk together the vinaigrette and orange juice concentrate until blended. Add the cabbage, oranges, apple, dried plums, celery, and scallions, tossing to evenly coat. Season to taste with pepper, if desired.

Sweet Blueberry Quesadillas

Ingredients:
10 ounces blueberries, frozen
¼ cup blueberries, fresh
1 cup apples, chopped
2 tablespoons sugar
4 8-inch tortillas, whole wheat
½ cup mozzarella cheese, part skim
½ cup ricotta cheese, fat-free
1 lemon, grated peel

Directions:
In saucepan combine frozen blueberries, apples and sugar. Bring to a boil over medium-high heat. Once you have reached a boil, reduce heat and simmer until fruit is soft (about 10 minutes). Purée fresh blueberries. Spread 1 tablespoon blueberry spread over each tortilla, leaving ½-inch border around. In bowl, combine cheeses with lemon peel. Spread ¼ of cheese mixture of one half of each tortilla. Add 2 tablespoons blueberry mixture to each quesadilla. Fold each tortilla over to enclose the filling. Heat large skillet over medium-high heat. Add quesadillas and cook until crisp and lightly browned on bottom. Turn and crisp on second side. To serve, place quesadillas on plates and top with remaining blueberry mixture.

Pink Lady Apple Salsa

Ingredients:

1 large tomato, cored and finely chopped
¾ cup finely chopped sweet onion
3 tablespoons freshly squeezed lime juice
1 large jalapeño chile, cored, seeded and finely chopped
2 Pink Lady apples
2 tablespoons minced fresh cilantro
1 tablespoon honey
Salt and freshly ground black pepper
Corn chips

Delicious as an appetizer served with corn chips, this salsa could also be spooned over a piece of grilled or baked halibut or other fish.

Directions:

Stir together the tomato, onion, lime juice and jalapeño in a medium bowl. Quarter and core the Pink Lady apples and cut them into fine dice. Stir the apples into the tomato mixture with the cilantro, honey and salt and pepper to taste. Refrigerate for up to 6 hours before serving. To serve, spoon the salsa into a serving bowl and serve with a bowl of corn chips alongside.

Spiced Apples

Ingredients:

6 medium apples, peeled and pared
1 cinnamon stick, broken into pieces
4 cloves
2 allspice
2 blades mace
½ teaspoon nutmeg
¾ cup brown sugar
½ cup apple cider

Directions:

Place peeled and pared apples in a casserole and then the stick of cinnamon, broken into pieces. Add cloves, allspice, blades of mace, nutmeg, brown sugar, and cider. Bake until tender and allow to cool. Serve them cold.

Indian Curry Sauce

Ingredients:

1 onion, chopped
1 apple, chopped
1 ounce butter
1 teaspoon mild curry powder
Juice of 1 lemon
Rind of 1 lemon, grated
1 pint water or stock
1 tablespoon seedless raisins
1 teaspoon flour (or more)
Salt

Directions:

Chop onion and apple and cook them in butter about 10 minutes, but do not let them brown. Add mild curry powder, the grated rind and juice of 1 lemon, the water or stock, some salt, the seedless raisins, and simmer until the onion is quite tender. Unless added to rice or paste, add small amount of flour to thicken after the onion and apple have cooked about 10 minutes.

Apple Canapés with Blue Cheese and Walnut

Ingredients:

8 ounces cream cheese, at room temperature
¾ cup finely crumbled blue cheese (about 3 oz.)
½ cup finely chopped toasted walnuts
1 tablespoon minced fresh chives
2 Red Delicious apples
Salt

Directions:

Put the cream cheese in a medium bowl and stir well to soften. Stir in the blue cheese, walnuts and chives until well blended. Season to taste with salt. Quarter and core the Red Delicious apples and cut them into ½-inch slices. Spread the walnut-blue cheese mixture over each slice of apple. Arrange the slices on a platter and serve.

Mashed Potatoes with Apples

Ingredients:
Potatoes, pared
Apples, cored and pared
Butter
Salt to taste

Directions:
Pare and cut up equal parts of potatoes and cored apples. Put the apples and potatoes into boiling water for five minutes and cook until tender. Drain and mash the potatoes and apples, and stir in a few tablespoonfuls of hot butter and salt.

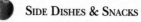

Apple and Raisin Filling for Duck

Ingredients:
1 pint finely chopped apples
½ cup seeded raisins
1½ cups bread crumbs
Sweet marjoram
2 tablespoons butter, melted
Salt and pepper to taste

Directions:
Chop enough apples fine to measure one pint. Add seeded raisins and breadcrumbs. Season with salt, pepper and sweet marjoram. Mix together with two tablespoons of melted butter. Pack into duck.

Spicy Apple and Pear Chutney

Ingredients:

1¾ cup finely diced Gala apples
1¾ cup finely diced Bartlett pears
2 tablespoons lemon juice
2 tablespoons chopped cilantro
1 clove garlic, finely chopped
½ cup finely chopped red onion
1½ teaspoons sugar
¼ teaspoon salt
¼ teaspoon red pepper flakes

This chutney is a great accompaniment to grilled fish, pork or poultry.

Directions:

Combine all ingredients. Chill at least 2 hours.

Honey Roasted Apples

(Courtesy of the National Honey Board)

Ingredients:

4 medium baking apples
½ cup honey
¼ cup orange juice
1 tablespoon lemon juice
1 teaspoon grated orange peel
½ teaspoon ground ginger (optional)
⅓ cup hot water

Directions:

Pare top ⅓ of apples and remove core leaving ½-inch of core on bottom. Place apples in oiled baking dish. Combine honey, orange juice, lemon juice, orange peel and ginger; mix well. Spoon over apples allowing mixture to fill centers and coat entire surface. Pour water into baking dish. Bake, covered, at 400°F for 15 minutes. Remove cover and bake 30 minutes longer or until apples are glazed and tender; baste with liquid from baking dish every 15 minutes. Microwave Method: Pare and core apples and mix glaze ingredients following directions above; omit water in pan. Arrange apples in a circle, ½-inch apart, in a microwave-safe pan. Cover tightly with plastic wrap. Microwave at high (100%) for 8 to 12 minutes (depending on size of apples) until apples are tender; baste apples and rotate dish every 2 to 3 minutes. Let stand 3 to 5 minutes before serving.

One teaspoon fresh grated or chopped candied ginger may be substituted.

Apple Snack Packs

Ingredients:

3 seconds cooking oil spray
2 cups Fuji Apples, peeled and sliced
½ teaspoon cinnamon
½ cup sweetened, dried cranberries
¼ cup sliced almonds, honey roasted

Directions:

Pre-heat oven to 250˚F. Spray cookie sheet with cooking oil. Slice apples into a shallow, flat cooking pan. Sprinkle with cinnamon and toss. Transfer coated apple slices to the greased cookie sheet and spread into a single layer. Place in the oven for 1 hour. Remove and cool. Combine cooked apples with sweetened, dried cranberries and sliced almonds. Place equal amounts in four re-sealable containers and refrigerate.

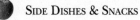

Potato Apple Dumplings

Ingredients:
White potatoes, pared
Flour
Apple, pared and cored

Directions:
Boil any quantity of white mealy potatoes; pare them, and mash them with a rolling-pin. Dredge in flour enough to form a dough, and roll it out to about the thickness of pie crust. Make up the dumplings by putting an apple, pared, cored, and quartered, inside each one. Boil them one hour.

Apple Snackster Stackers

(Courtesy of the National Honey Board)

Ingredients:

¾ cup chunky peanut butter
⅓ cup honey
4 large Granny Smith or Red Delicious apples, stems removed
4 small sprigs fresh mint, optional
Cold water
Lemon juice

Directions:

In a small bowl, mix peanut butter and honey together until well blended. Set aside. Fill a large bowl with cold water and stir in lemon juice. Set aside.

Use an apple corer to remove the center of the apple, making a hollow space from stem end through the bottom. With a sharp knife, cut apple crosswise into 4 thick slices. Dip apple slices in lemon water and gently pat dry with paper towels. Starting with the bottom piece, use a butter knife to spread the peanut butter mixture on the cut sides of each slice and gently press them

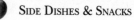

Columbia Chutney

Ingredients:
15 large sour apples, pared and chopped fine
2 onions, chopped
1 cup seeded raisins, chopped
1 quart vinegar
2 cups brown sugar
2 tablespoons mustard seed
2 tablespoons ginger
2 tablespoons salt

Directions:
Put sour apples (pared and chopped fine), 2 onions (chopped), and seeded raisins (chopped) all in a kettle, and pour vinegar over it. Let it simmer for 2 hours. Then add the brown sugar, mustard seed, ginger, and salt, and boil slowly one hour more. While hot, put in air tight jars and seal. Keep in cool dark place.

Apple Dippers with Honey and Peanut Butter

(Courtesy of the National Honey Board)

Ingredients:

¾ cup chunky peanut butter

⅓ cup honey

4 large Granny Smith or Red Delicious apples, stems removed

cold water

lemon juice

Directions:

In a small bowl, mix peanut butter and honey together until well blended. Set aside. Fill a large bowl with cold water and stir in lemon juice. Set aside.

With a sharp knife, cut each apple in half from stem end to bottom. Cut each half into 4 to 6 wedges. With knife or melon ballet remove apple core from each wedge. Dip wedges in lemon water and gently pat dry with paper towels. Spoon the peanut butter mixture into a small bowl and surround with apple wedges for dipping.

Beverages

Apple Ball Cocktail

Ingredients:

8 apples
Juice of 1 lemon
1 teaspoon salt
¼ pound (1 cup) white grapes
⅓ cup maraschino cherries
3 tablespoons syrup from cherries
Juice of ½ orange
Water

Directions:

Cut tops from stem end of the apples. Remove inside of apples with a French ball cutter, putting balls in 2 cups cold water with the lemon juice. Put the apple shells in 1 quart cold water to which is added 1 teaspoon salt. Remove skins and seeds from the white grapes. Just before serving drain apple shells. Remove apple balls from the water. Drain and mix with the white grapes and maraschino cherries and fill apple shells. Mix syrup from maraschino cherries with the orange juice and pour over the apple balls. Serve apple shells in individual dishes or cocktail glasses surrounded with crushed ice.

Apple may be removed in small oval shapes with a coffee spoon, if a French ball cutter is not available.

Hot Honey Cider
(Courtesy of the National Honey Board)

Ingredients:
1 gallon fresh apple cider
1 cup honey
½ cup orange juice
Juice of ½ lemon
6 to 7 cinnamon sticks
1 tablespoon whole cloves
½ teaspoon allspice
1 apple
1 orange
1 cup dark rum, optional

Directions:
Add cider, honey, orange juice, lemon juice, cinnamon sticks, cloves and allspice to a 2-gallon pot. Simmer on medium-low heat for 1 hour. Slice apple and orange into about 6 slices each, leaving the core and peels, and add to pot. Add rum. Serve warm.

Veggie Delight Smoothie

Ingredients:

2 cups apple juice
1 cup sliced apple
1 cup applesauce
1 cup sliced carrots
1 cup peeled and sliced cucumber
2½ cups ice

Directions:

Place all items into blender and blend until smooth. Serve immediately.

Apple Toddy

Ingredients:
Cider brandy (applejack)
½ apple, baked
Water
1 teaspoon white sugar
Grated nutmeg

Directions:
Dissolve 1 large teaspoonful of fine white sugar in a little boiling water. Pour into a hot bar-glass (middle-sized), and add 1 wineglassful of cider brandy (applejack) and half of a baked apple. Then fill the glass two-thirds full of boiling water, stir well, powder the top with grated nutmeg, and serve with a spoon.

Fruit and Honey Punch

(Courtesy of the National Honey Board)

Ingredients:

2 cups fresh apple cider
2 cups cranberry juice
¼ cup honey
1 cinnamon stick
4 slices lemon
4 whole cloves

Tip:

One to two cups of dry red wine can be added.

Directions:

Combine all ingredients in saucepan; heat only until mixture boils. Pour into serving glasses or mugs; serve immediately.

Triple-Fruit Smoothie

Ingredients:

8 ounces apple-cranberry juice
1½ cups fresh applesauce
1 small banana, sliced
4 ounces vanilla flavored soy or
Rice milk, low-fat

Directions:

In a blender, combine all the ingredients and purée until thick
and smooth. Pour into glasses and serve.

Apple Punch

Ingredients:
Apples, sliced
Lemons, sliced
Powdered sugar
1 bottle claret

Directions:
Slice apples and lemons and lay in alternate layers in a china bowl, covering each layer thickly with powdered sugar, until the bowl is about half filled. Pour a bottle of claret over it and let stand six hours. After pouring through a muslin bag, it is ready for use.

Desserts

Apple Dumplings

Ingredients:

2 tablespoons firmly packed light brown sugar
1½ teaspoons cinnamon
1 teaspoon cornstarch
1 teaspoon vanilla extract
6 small apples, peeled and cored
6 square 7-inch egg roll wrappers
Nonstick cooking spray

Directions:

Preheat the oven to 375°F. Spray six muffin cups with nonstick cooking spray. In a large bowl, combine the sugar, cinnamon, cornstarch, vanilla, and 1 tablespoon water. Roll peeled apples in the mixture until coated. Place one apple in the center of each egg roll wrapper. Bring the corners up to the top of the apple, pressing and folding to seal the edges. Place each dumpling in a muffin cup and lightly spray the tops with nonstick cooking spray. Bake until golden, about 20 minutes. Cool on a rack 15 minutes; serve warm.

Apple Strudel

Ingredients:

Apples, pared
Cinnamon and sugar, mixed
1 cup sugar
1 teaspoon baking powder
1 cup flour
½ teaspoon salt
1 egg

Directions:

Into bottom of a buttered baking dish put thick layers of apples. Sprinkle with sugar and cinnamon mixed. Dot with lumps of butter.

Into a mixing bowl sift the sugar, baking powder, flour, and salt. Into this break 1 egg. Mix until crumbly. Put over apples and bake in moderate oven (350°F) until crust is brown. Serve with milk, whipped cream or ice cream.

Apple Coffee Cake

(Courtesy of NHLBI, part of NIH and HHS)

Ingredients:

5 cups tart apples, cored,
peeled, chopped
1 cup sugar
1 cup dark raisins
½ cup pecans, chopped
¼ cup vegetable oil
2 teaspoons vanilla
1 egg, beaten
2½ cups sifted all-purpose flour
1½ teaspoons baking soda
2 teaspoons ground cinnamon

Apples and raisins provide
the moistness, which means
less oil can be used in
this low saturated fat, low
cholesterol, and low-sodium
coffee cake.

Directions:

Preheat oven to 350°F. Lightly oil a 13 x 9 x 2-inch pan. In
a large mixing bowl, combine apples with sugar, raisins, and
pecans; mix well. Let stand 30 minutes. Stir in oil, vanilla, and
egg. Sift together flour, soda, and cinnamon; stir into apple mixture about ⅓ at a time just enough to moisten dry ingredients.
Turn batter into pan. Bake 35 to 40 minutes. Cool cake slightly
before serving.

Apple Ring Fritters

Ingredients:

1 cup sifted flour
1½ teaspoons baking powder
2 tablespoons sugar
½ teaspoon salt
¾ cup milk
1 egg
4 large apples

Directions:

Sift dry ingredients. Add milk and egg. Beat well. Peel and core apples and slice in rings about ¼-inch thick. Dip rings in batter and drop into skillet containing ½-inch of hot melted shortening. Fry until golden brown on both sides. Drain on paper towel. Mix sugar and cinnamon together and sprinkle over fritters. Makes 16 to 20.

Apple and Peach Conserve

Ingredients:
2 cups apples, chopped
2 cups peaches, chopped
Juice of 2 lemons
3 cups sugar

Directions:
Use tart unpeeled apples and firm ripe peaches, cut into small pieces. Combine with lemon juice and sugar. Cook slowly until the apple is transparent (about 20 minutes). Pour into sterilized glass jars and seal.

Apple Butter

Ingredients:
4 quarts apples
2 quarts apple cider
2 cups sugar
2 cups dark corn syrup
1 teaspoon cinnamon

Directions:
Boil the cider until reduced to 1 quart. Pare the apples and slice thin. Put the apples into the cider and cook very slowly, stirring frequently, until it begins to thicken. Add sugar, syrup and cinnamon and continue to cook until thick enough to spread when cool. Seal in sterilized jars. Makes 5 to 6 pints.

Simple Applesauce

Ingredients:

4 large apples, any variety, preferably sweet
½ cup water
½ teaspoon cinnamon

Sweet apples will not require sugar. If tart apples are used, some sugar may be needed.

Directions:

Core, but do not peel apples; cut into chunks. Add water and bring to boil. Reduce heat to low and simmer 25 minutes or until apples are soft. Add cinnamon and cook for 5 minutes. Cool. Place in blender and blend until smooth.

Honey Yogurt Dumplings
with Apples

(Courtesy of the National Honey Board)

Ingredients:

Dumpling batter:

1 cup all-purpose flour
4 teaspoons baking powder
1 teaspoon ground cinnamon
⅛ teaspoon salt
1 egg
6 tablespoons low-fat plain yogurt
1 tablespoon honey
1 tablespoon 2% low-fat milk
1 teaspoon grated orange peel

Apple mixture:

4 cups apple slices
2 cups cranberry juice
½ cup honey
1 cinnamon stick or ¼ teaspoon ground cinnamon
¼ teaspoon ground nutmeg

Directions:

Combine flour, baking powder, cinnamon and salt in large bowl. Mix together egg, yogurt, 1 tablespoon honey, milk and orange peel in separate large bowl; stir into flour mixture to form moist batter. Combine apples, juice, remaining ½ cup honey, cinnamon stick and nutmeg in heavy large skillet; mix well. Bring to a boil over medium-high heat. Reduce heat to low. Drop tablespoonfuls of batter over hot apple mixture. Cover and simmer 15 to 20 minutes or until dumplings are cooked through and wooden pick inserted near dumpling center comes out clean.

Italian Fruit Cobbler
with Vanilla Sauce

Ingredients:

4 Bartlett pears, peeled, cored, and sliced
3 Granny Smith apples, peeled, cored and sliced
½ cup dried cranberries
1 tablespoon all-purpose flour
1 tablespoon sugar
2 ounces orange juice
1 cup all-purpose flour
⅓ cup polenta or yellow cornmeal

¼ cup sugar
1 teaspoon cinnamon, ground
4 ounces low-fat cream cheese at room temperature
3 tablespoons ice cold water
1 (8 oz.) container fat-free vanilla yogurt
4 ounces fat-free half-and-half
Sugar and ground cinnamon for sprinkling

Directions:

Preheat oven to 375°F.

Filling:

In a large bowl, combine first six ingredients and toss until mixed well. Spoon into an ungreased 9 x 13-inch baking dish.

Topping:

In a medium bowl, whisk together the flour, polenta, sugar and cinnamon. With a pastry blender or two knives used scissor-fashion, cut in the cream cheese until the mixture resembles baby peas. Sprinkle in the ice water, 1 tablespoon at a time, mixing lightly with a fork after each addition, to form a dry dough that holds together. Carefully spread the dough on top of the fruit and sprinkle with a little sugar and cinnamon.

Bake the cobbler for 40 to 50 minutes, or until the filling is bubbling and the topping is golden.

Meanwhile, in a small bowl, whisk together the sauce ingredients (yogurt and half & half). To serve, drizzle the sauce in a circle pattern on each plate and top with a portion of the warm cobbler.

Apple Koker

Ingredients:

4 large sour apples
¼ cup butter
1 egg
¾ cup milk
2 cups flour, sifted
½ teaspoon salt
2 teaspoons baking powder
2 tablespoons sugar

Lemon sauce:
1 cup sugar
3 teaspoons corn starch
2 cups water, boiling
Rind of 1 lemon, grated
Juice of 1 lemon
1 tablespoon butter

Directions:

Mix salt and baking powder with two cups of sifted flour. Add butter. Beat one egg light, add three-fourths cup of milk, and stir into the flour. Use more milk if needed to make dough soft enough to spread ½-inch on a shallow baking pan. Pare, quarter and core four large sour apples, and divide each quarter lengthwise. Lay them in parallel rows on top of the dough, core edge down, and press them into the dough slightly. Sprinkle two tablespoons of sugar over the apples, and bake in a hot oven twenty minutes. Turn it out, apple side up, on a hollow platter, and serve with lemon sauce.

Lemon sauce:

Mix well the corn starch and sugar in a saucepan. Add two cups of boiling water, stir well and cook ten minutes. Add the grated rind and juice and one tablespoon of butter.

Banana-Apple Sherbet

Ingredients:

2 large ripe bananas
1 tablespoon fresh lemon juice
1½ cups fresh applesauce
3 tablespoons honey

Directions:

Cut the bananas into 1-inch-thick slices; dip in the lemon juice
to prevent browning. Arrange the bananas on a baking sheet.
Place in the freezer for about 4 hours, or until firm. Pour the
applesauce into an ice cube tray. Place in the freezer for about 4
hours, or until firm. In a food processor or blender, combine the
frozen bananas and applesauce and purée until almost smooth.
Add the honey and process until smooth and creamy. Scoop into
serving dishes and serve immediately.

Apple Honey Crisp with Warm Nutmeg Cream

(Courtesy of the National Honey Board)

Ingredients:

Apple honey crisp:
2 pounds apples, quartered
and sliced (1½ quarts)
½ cup plus ¼ cup honey,
(separated)
1 teaspoon cinnamon
½ teaspoon nutmeg
1 cup flour
¼ cup butter, softened

Warm nutmeg cream:
½ cup whipping cream
2 tablespoons honey
2 tablespoons butter
¼ teaspoon nutmeg

Directions:

Apple honey crisp:

Toss apples with ½ cup honey, cinnamon and nutmeg in bowl. Turn into 2-quart baking dish. For topping, beat flour with butter and ¼ cup honey until crumbly; sprinkle over apples. Bake at 350°F for 40 to 45 minutes or until apples are tender and topping is golden. Serve with Warm Nutmeg Cream.

Warm nutmeg cream:

Combine all ingredients in saucepan and bring to boil. Simmer, stirring often, for 5 minutes or until mixture thickens slightly.

Apple Bread Pudding

Ingredients:

3 cups half-and-half
1 cup packed brown sugar
4 eggs
1 teaspoon vanilla extract
½ teaspoon ground cinnamon
¼ teaspoon ground nutmeg
6 cups ¾-inch cubes day old bread
2 Golden Delicious apples

Directions:

Preheat the oven to 350°F. Generously butter a 2-quart baking dish. Warm the half-and-half over medium heat, add the brown sugar and stir until dissolved; set aside. Whisk the eggs in a medium bowl until well blended. Slowly whisk in the half-and-half, vanilla extract, cinnamon and nutmeg. Put the bread cubes in a large bowl. Quarter and core the Golden Delicious apples, cut them into ½-inch cubes and add to the bread cubes. Pour the egg mixture over, stir and let sit for 5 minutes, stirring occasionally. Transfer the bread pudding mixture to the prepared baking dish. Bake until the custard is set and the top is nicely browned, about 45 minutes. Let sit for 15 to 20 minutes before serving.

Resources

Resources for Finding Local Farms, Farmstands, and Sustainable Food Organizations

Local Harvest

www.localharvest.org

Use the search tool provided by the Local Harvest website to find farmers' markets, co-ops, farms, and other sustainable food sources in your local area.

Eat Well Guide

www.eatwellguide.org

The Eat Well Guide offers a comprehensive search of local organizations, farms, farmers markets, restaurants, and co-ops that offer local, organic, and sustainable food.

Local.com

www.local.com

Search for local fruit and vegetables stands, farms, organizations and more on this website.

All About Apples

www.allaboutapples.com/orchard/index.htm

All About Apples provides a list of apple orchards in each state.

State and Regional Apple Growers Associations and Groups

California Apple Commission
www.calapples.org

Connecticut Apple Marketing Board
www.ctapples.com

Michigan Apple Committee
www.michiganapples.com

Minnesota Apple Growers Association
www.minnesotaapple.org

New York Apple Country
www.nyapplecountry.com

Ohio Apples
www.ohioapples.com

Pennsylvania Apples
www.pennsylvaniaapples.org

United Fresh Produce Association
www.unitedfresh.org

U.S. Apple Association
www.usapple.org

Virginia State Apple Board
www.virginiaapples.org

Vermont Apples
www.vermontapples.org

Washington Apples
www.bestapples.com

Acknowledgments

Hatherleigh Press would like to extend a special thank you to Jo Brielyn and Christina Anger—without your hard work and creativity this book would not have been possible.

My Recipes

My Recipes

My Recipes